Beyond Screens:
The Next Generation of User Interfaces

By

Kendra H. Thurston

TABLE OF CONTENTS

Introduction

A. Importance of user interfaces in modern technology

User interfaces play a vital role in our modern technology-driven world. From smartphones and tablets to laptops and smart TVs, user interfaces are the gateway through which we interact with and harness the power of technology. They serve as the bridge between humans and machines, facilitating seamless communication and enabling us to access a wide range of digital services and functionalities.

The importance of user interfaces cannot be overstated. They have the power to make or break the user experience, shaping our interactions with technology and influencing our overall satisfaction and productivity. Well-designed interfaces can enhance efficiency, streamline workflows, and empower users to effortlessly navigate complex systems. On the other hand, poorly designed or clunky interfaces can lead to frustration, confusion, and even abandonment of the technology altogether.

In the past, screens have been the predominant medium for user interfaces. From the early days of cathode ray tubes (CRTs) to the advent of flat-panel displays and touchscreens, screens have revolutionized the way we interact with technology. However, as our digital landscape continues to evolve at a rapid pace, the limitations of screen-based interfaces are becoming increasingly evident.

One of the key limitations of screen-based interfaces is the inherent restriction on interaction. Users are typically confined to touch or click-based input, limiting the range of possible interactions and constraining the potential for immersive experiences. Additionally, screens often demand visual attention, diverting our focus from the physical world and sometimes causing information overload.

Moreover, the rapid integration of technology into various aspects of our lives, such as augmented reality, smart homes, and wearable devices, calls for new and innovative approaches to user interfaces. The next generation of user interfaces needs to go beyond screens and explore alternative technologies that can provide more natural, intuitive, and immersive interactions.

In this book, "Beyond Screens: The Next Generation of User Interfaces," we will embark on a journey to explore the future of user interfaces. We will delve into emerging technologies such as gesture-based interfaces, voice-controlled interfaces, haptic feedback, augmented reality, mixed reality, brain-computer interfaces, and more. By understanding these technologies and their potential, we can envision a future where our interactions with technology are seamless, immersive, and responsive to our needs.

Through this exploration, we aim to inspire designers, developers, and researchers to push the boundaries of user interfaces, driving innovation and creating transformative experiences for users. By embracing the next generation of user interfaces, we can unlock new possibilities, enhance productivity, and reshape the way we interact with technology in a manner that is more intuitive, engaging, and human-centric.

Join us on this exciting journey as we venture into the realm of the next generation of user interfaces, where screens are just the beginning, and where technology seamlessly integrates into our lives, enhancing our experiences and shaping a brighter future.

B. Evolution of screens as primary user interfaces

Introduction: User interfaces have come a long way since the early days of computing, and screens have played a central role in their evolution. From humble monochrome displays to vibrant, high-resolution touchscreens, screens have become the primary medium through which we interact with technology. This chapter explores the fascinating journey of screens as user interfaces and sets the stage for the next generation of interfaces.

The evolution of screens as primary user interfaces has been marked by significant milestones and transformative advancements. In the early days of computing, screens were primarily text-based, displaying monospaced characters on a black background. These

8

rudimentary interfaces required users to input commands using keyboards and navigate through complex command-line interfaces.

As technology progressed, so did the capabilities of screens. The introduction of graphical user interfaces (GUIs) revolutionized the way we interacted with computers. Graphical elements, icons, and windows brought a new level of intuitiveness and visual appeal to the user experience. Familiar metaphors such as the desktop, folders, and files made computing more accessible to a broader audience.

The advent of color displays further enhanced the visual richness of user interfaces, providing a more engaging and immersive experience. With the proliferation of personal computers, screens became more affordable and widespread, making graphical interfaces the norm rather than the exception.

The rise of mobile devices brought about a paradigm shift in user interfaces. Compact screens coupled with touch-sensitive technology allowed for direct manipulation and intuitive gestures. The introduction of multi-touch screens opened up new possibilities for interaction, enabling pinch-to-zoom, swipe gestures, and more. Mobile apps and responsive design became essential in tailoring interfaces for smaller screens and diverse device form factors.

In recent years, screens have not only become more advanced in terms of resolution and color reproduction but have also evolved in shape and form. Curved screens, edge-to-edge displays, and foldable screens are pushing the boundaries of design and providing new avenues for interaction.

However, as screens have become ubiquitous, we have also encountered their limitations. Screen fatigue, eye strain, and information overload have become common concerns. There is a growing realization that relying solely on screens as user interfaces may not be sustainable or optimal for all applications and contexts.

Hence, the time has come to explore the next generation of user interfaces that go beyond screens. This book aims to delve into alternative technologies that can complement or replace screens, offering new ways to interact with technology. By examining the challenges and opportunities presented by these emerging interfaces, we can pave the way for a more diverse, inclusive, and immersive user experience.

In the following chapters, we will explore technologies such as gesture-based interfaces, voice-controlled interfaces, augmented reality, mixed reality, haptic feedback, brain-computer interfaces, adaptive interfaces, and more. Together, let us embark on this journey to unlock the potential of the next generation of user interfaces and shape the future of human-computer interaction.

C. Need for the next generation of user interfaces

Introduction: The rapid advancement of technology has transformed the way we live, work, and interact with the world around us. As our reliance on technology continues to grow, so does the need for more advanced and intuitive user interfaces. This chapter explores the pressing need for the next generation of user interfaces and highlights the shortcomings of current interface technologies.

The current landscape of user interfaces predominantly revolves around screens, such as those found on smartphones, tablets, computers, and TVs. While screens have undoubtedly revolutionized our interactions with technology, they have limitations that hinder the full potential of human-computer interaction.

One of the primary challenges with screen-based interfaces is their lack of naturalness. Interacting with screens often requires manual input through touch, mouse clicks, or keyboard strokes. While these methods have served us well, they do not fully align with our innate human tendencies for natural and intuitive interaction. We are wired to use gestures, speech, and even our thoughts to communicate and manipulate the world around us. The next generation of user interfaces needs to bridge this gap, enabling more natural and effortless interactions.

Another limitation of current interfaces is the dependency on visual attention. Screen-based interfaces demand our constant visual focus, often causing distractions and information overload. In an increasingly multitasking-oriented society, this demand for visual attention can impede productivity and lead to cognitive strain. The next generation of interfaces should alleviate these challenges by providing alternative sensory channels that distribute the cognitive load more effectively.

Furthermore, the surge of emerging technologies, such as augmented reality, virtual reality, artificial intelligence, and the Internet of Things, necessitates interfaces that can seamlessly integrate and harness their potential. Current screen-based interfaces often struggle to fully leverage these technologies, hindering their widespread adoption and limiting the scope of user experiences. The next generation of interfaces should provide more immersive and context-aware interactions, enabling users to navigate and control these complex technological ecosystems effortlessly.

Moreover, the need for accessible and inclusive interfaces has become increasingly crucial. Screen-based interfaces, while widely used, can present barriers for individuals with disabilities or impairments. The next generation of interfaces must prioritize universal design principles to ensure that everyone, regardless of their abilities, can participate fully in the digital world.

In this book, "Beyond Screens: The Next Generation of User Interfaces," we will explore alternative interface technologies that address these needs and push the boundaries of human-computer interaction. By embracing new modalities, such as gesture recognition, voice commands, haptic feedback, brain-computer interfaces, and adaptive interfaces, we can create interfaces that are more intuitive, engaging, and accessible to a broader range of users.

Join us on this journey as we delve into the challenges, opportunities, and possibilities presented by the next generation of user interfaces.

Chapter 1
Exploring Limitations of Current User Interfaces

A. Challenges posed by traditional screen-based interfaces

While screens have been the primary interface medium for decades, they are not without their limitations. Traditional screen-based interfaces present a range of challenges that hinder the user experience and limit the potential of human-computer interaction.

One major challenge is the inherent limitation of interaction. Screen-based interfaces primarily rely on touch or mouse-based input, restricting the types of interactions users can perform. Although touchscreens have introduced greater flexibility, they still largely revolve around tapping, swiping, and pinching gestures. This limited set of interactions can be insufficient for complex tasks, creative expression, or precise control.

Additionally, screen-based interfaces often suffer from a lack of tactile feedback. Users do not receive physical responses or haptic sensations when interacting with virtual elements on a screen. This absence of tactile feedback can make it challenging to gauge the success of an action or interact with virtual objects in a natural and intuitive manner.

The visual-centric nature of screen-based interfaces also poses challenges. Constantly staring at screens can lead to eye strain, fatigue, and discomfort, particularly during extended usage. Moreover, the increasing reliance on screens in our daily lives can result in excessive screen time, affecting overall well-being and cognitive health.

Furthermore, screen-based interfaces demand users' undivided visual attention. This requirement can be problematic in situations where multitasking or maintaining awareness of the physical surroundings is crucial. For instance, using a smartphone while walking or operating a vehicle poses significant safety risks due to the distraction caused by screen-focused interactions.

The limitations of screen-based interfaces become even more apparent in certain application domains. Industries such as healthcare, aviation, and manufacturing often require specialized interfaces that provide real-time data, precise control, and seamless integration with complex systems. Traditional screens may fall short in meeting these specific requirements, resulting in suboptimal user experiences and potential safety hazards.

As technology continues to advance and permeate various aspects of our lives, it is imperative to recognize and address these limitations. The next generation of user interfaces must go beyond screens and explore alternative modalities that offer more diverse, intuitive, and immersive interaction possibilities. By acknowledging and understanding the challenges posed by traditional screen-based interfaces, we can set the stage for the exploration of innovative solutions and pave the way for the evolution of user interfaces.

In the subsequent chapters, we will delve into emerging interface technologies that aim to overcome these limitations. Through this exploration, we hope to uncover new approaches, inspire innovation, and shape a future where user interfaces seamlessly blend with our natural tendencies, enabling us to interact with technology in a more seamless, intuitive, and holistic manner.

B. Issues related to limited interaction and engagement

While screens have become the prevalent form of user interfaces, they often impose limitations on the depth of interaction and level of engagement users can achieve. These limitations give rise to various issues that impact the overall user experience and hinder the potential of human-computer interaction.

One significant issue is the limited range of interactions offered by screen-based interfaces. Traditional screens primarily rely on touch, mouse clicks, or keyboard inputs, constraining the types of actions users can perform. This limited interaction repertoire can be particularly restrictive when dealing with complex tasks or creative endeavors that require more nuanced and expressive interactions.

The lack of physicality in screen-based interfaces also contributes to a sense of disconnection and reduced engagement. Users are unable to physically manipulate objects or experience tactile feedback when interacting with virtual elements on a screen. This absence of haptic sensations and physical presence can diminish the level of immersion and make interactions feel less tangible and satisfying.

Moreover, screen-based interfaces often lack dynamic and adaptive elements that can cater to individual user preferences and needs. These interfaces tend to provide a one-size-fits-all approach, offering limited personalization or customization options. As a result, users may feel detached or disengaged from the interface, leading to a suboptimal user experience and reduced productivity.

Another issue lies in the limited opportunities for natural and intuitive interaction. Screen-based interfaces often require users to adapt to the interface's constraints and learn specific gestures or commands to interact effectively. This learning curve can create a barrier for new users or those less familiar with technology. Additionally, the lack of natural interaction can impede

19

the seamless integration of technology into our daily lives, hindering the fluidity of human-computer interaction.

Furthermore, the visual-centric nature of screen-based interfaces can lead to cognitive overload and information overload. Users are bombarded with an overwhelming amount of visual stimuli, which can result in reduced attention span, increased mental fatigue, and difficulty in processing information efficiently. This, in turn, affects engagement and can lead to decreased productivity and user satisfaction.

To overcome these issues, the next generation of user interfaces must explore alternative modalities that enable richer and more engaging interactions. Gesture-based interfaces, voice-controlled interfaces, haptic feedback, and immersive technologies such as augmented reality and virtual reality hold promise in providing more intuitive, expressive, and immersive interactions. By addressing the limitations related to limited interaction and engagement, these emerging interfaces have the potential to revolutionize user experiences and unlock new possibilities for human-computer interaction.

In the following chapters, we will delve deeper into these alternative interface technologies and their potential to overcome the limitations we have discussed. Through understanding and embracing these advancements, we can design interfaces that foster deeper engagement, enhance productivity, and create more meaningful and satisfying interactions between users and technology.

C. User experience shortcomings and potential frustrations

While screens have become ubiquitous in our digital lives, they are not immune to user experience shortcomings and potential frustrations. The limitations and design choices inherent in current screen-based interfaces can give rise to various challenges that impact user satisfaction and hinder the seamless interaction between humans and technology.

One notable user experience shortcoming is the steep learning curve associated with many screen-based interfaces. Navigating complex menus, understanding intricate hierarchies, and memorizing various gestures or commands can be overwhelming for new users. This learning process can lead to frustration, confusion, and decreased engagement, especially when the interface fails to provide clear guidance or intuitive feedback.

Another source of frustration lies in the lack of responsiveness and feedback provided by screen-based interfaces. Users often expect instantaneous and fluid interactions, but delays, lags, and unresponsive elements can disrupt the flow and degrade the overall user experience. Additionally, the absence of tactile feedback or physical affordances can make it difficult to perceive whether an action has been successfully executed, leading to uncertainty and potential errors.

Screen-based interfaces are also susceptible to issues related to information overload. The presentation of excessive or poorly organized information can overwhelm users and impede their ability to locate relevant content or perform desired tasks efficiently. This overload of visual stimuli can strain cognitive resources, hinder decision-making processes, and detract from the overall user experience.

Furthermore, the lack of contextual awareness in screen-based interfaces can contribute to frustration and decreased efficiency. Many interfaces fail to adapt dynamically to users' needs, preferences, or situational contexts. As a result, users may find themselves repeatedly performing unnecessary actions, dealing with cluttered interfaces, or struggling to locate relevant features. This lack of adaptability can hinder productivity and impede the seamless integration of technology into users' lives.

Accessibility is another important aspect where screen-based interfaces often fall short. Users with disabilities or impairments may encounter barriers when trying to interact with these interfaces. Insufficient support for assistive technologies, poor contrast, limited customization options, and inaccessible design choices can create frustrations and exclude individuals from fully participating in the digital realm.

To address these user experience shortcomings and potential frustrations, the next generation of user interfaces should prioritize intuitive design, responsiveness, adaptability, contextual awareness, and inclusivity. By leveraging emerging technologies and exploring alternative interface modalities, such as voice control, gesture recognition, haptic feedback, and adaptive interfaces, we can create interfaces that are more user-centric, responsive, and tailored to individual needs.

In the subsequent chapters, we will delve into these alternative interface technologies and examine their potential to overcome the user experience shortcomings and frustrations associated with current screen-based interfaces.

Chapter 2
Rise of Alternative User Interface Technologies

A. Introduction to emerging interface technologies

As the limitations of traditional screen-based interfaces become increasingly evident, the world of user interfaces is witnessing a rise in alternative technologies that offer new possibilities for interaction and engagement. This chapter serves as an introduction to these emerging interface technologies, exploring their fundamental concepts and highlighting their potential to reshape the way we interact with technology.

One prominent category of emerging interface technologies is gesture-based interfaces. These interfaces enable users to interact with devices and systems through natural and intuitive gestures, such as waving, pointing, or swiping. By capturing and interpreting these gestures, devices can translate them into meaningful commands or actions. Gesture-based interfaces eliminate the need for physical touch or reliance on peripheral devices like keyboards or mice, fostering a more direct and immersive form of interaction.

Another exciting technology on the horizon is voice-controlled interfaces. Voice recognition and natural language processing algorithms empower users to interact with devices using spoken commands or queries. This technology allows for hands-free operation, making it particularly useful in scenarios where manual input is challenging or undesirable, such as when driving or multitasking. Voice-controlled interfaces have the potential to enhance accessibility, provide seamless integration with smart home devices, and enable efficient information retrieval through voice-based assistants.

Haptic feedback is another area that holds promise for revolutionizing user interfaces. By leveraging tactile sensations, haptic feedback interfaces provide users with physical feedback and touch sensations in response to their actions. This technology enhances the sense of realism and engagement, enabling users to feel the texture, shape, or resistance of virtual objects. Haptic feedback can be applied through vibration motors, force sensors, or even more advanced technologies like electroactive polymers, opening up new possibilities for immersive and tactile interactions.

The emergence of augmented reality (AR) and mixed reality (MR) interfaces has garnered significant attention in recent years. These interfaces blend digital content with the physical environment, allowing users to perceive and interact with virtual objects in real-time. AR overlays digital information onto the user's view of the real world, while MR interfaces seamlessly integrate virtual and real elements, enabling users to interact with both simultaneously. These technologies have the potential to transform industries such as gaming, education, healthcare, and design, offering immersive experiences and enhancing productivity.

Brain-computer interfaces (BCIs) represent another frontier in user interface technology. BCIs establish a direct communication pathway between the brain and external devices, allowing users to control technology through neural signals. By detecting and interpreting brain activity, BCIs enable users to interact with devices or systems using their thoughts, opening up possibilities for individuals with mobility impairments or offering new modes of interaction beyond traditional input methods.

These emerging interface technologies are reshaping the landscape of human-computer interaction, expanding the range of possibilities and paving the way for more natural, intuitive, and immersive experiences. In the following chapters, we will delve deeper into each of these technologies, exploring their principles, applications, and potential impact on the next generation of user interfaces. By understanding and embracing these emerging technologies, we can shape a future where interactions with technology are more seamless, intuitive, and responsive to our needs and desires.

B. Gesture-based interfaces and their advantages

Gesture-based interfaces have emerged as a compelling alternative to traditional screen-based interactions, offering a more natural and intuitive way to interact with technology. This section explores the concept of gesture-based interfaces and highlights their advantages in enhancing user experiences and expanding the possibilities of human-computer interaction.

Gesture-based interfaces enable users to interact with devices or systems through physical gestures, mimicking natural movements and behaviors. By capturing and interpreting these gestures, devices can understand user intentions and translate them into meaningful actions. This technology eliminates the need for physical touch or reliance on external input devices, promoting a more direct and immersive form of interaction.

One of the primary advantages of gesture-based interfaces is their intuitive nature. Gestures are ingrained in our everyday lives as a means of communication and expression. By leveraging familiar gestures, such as waving, pointing, or swiping, gesture-based interfaces enable users to interact with technology using actions that feel instinctive and effortless. This intuitiveness reduces the learning curve associated with new interfaces, making them more accessible to a broader range of users.

Another advantage of gesture-based interfaces is the potential for enhanced spatial interactions. Unlike screen-based interfaces that are confined to a two-dimensional plane, gesture-based interfaces introduce the concept of three-dimensional interactions. Users can manipulate virtual objects or navigate through virtual spaces by physically moving their hands or bodies. This spatial awareness adds a new layer of immersion and engagement to user experiences, particularly in applications such as virtual reality or augmented reality.

Gesture-based interfaces also offer the advantage of increased mobility and flexibility. By eliminating the need for physical contact with a device, users are liberated from stationary positions and can interact with technology in more dynamic and fluid ways. This mobility is especially valuable in scenarios where manual dexterity or physical limitations may pose challenges. Users can control devices or systems from a distance or while on the move, providing a greater sense of freedom and convenience.

Furthermore, gesture-based interfaces can foster a more natural and expressive form of interaction. Users can convey meaning or intent through gestures that closely resemble real-world actions or behaviors. This expressive potential allows for more nuanced interactions, enabling users to communicate subtle variations in movement or convey complex commands through a single gesture. By aligning with our innate human tendencies for non-verbal communication, gesture-based interfaces can enhance the richness and depth of user interactions.

Gesture-based interfaces are finding applications in various domains, including gaming, fitness, automotive, and smart home control. From intuitive hand gestures to full-body movements, these interfaces are revolutionizing the way we interact with technology, offering a more immersive, seamless, and user-centric experience.

In the subsequent chapters, we will delve deeper into the implementation, challenges, and future possibilities of gesture-based interfaces. By understanding and harnessing the advantages of gesture-based interactions, we can unlock new opportunities for innovation, creativity, and user empowerment. Together, let us explore the exciting potential of gesture-based interfaces and their role in shaping the next generation of user interfaces.

C. Voice-controlled interfaces and their potential

Voice-controlled interfaces have emerged as a powerful and intuitive way for users to interact with technology. This section explores the concept of voice-controlled interfaces and highlights their potential to revolutionize user experiences and transform the landscape of human-computer interaction.

Voice-controlled interfaces enable users to interact with devices or systems using spoken commands or queries. By leveraging voice recognition and natural language processing technologies, these interfaces can understand and interpret the user's spoken words, translating them into meaningful actions or responses. This hands-free and conversational approach to interaction offers a range of advantages and opens up new possibilities for a diverse range of users.

One of the key advantages of voice-controlled interfaces is their natural and intuitive nature. Speech is one of the most fundamental modes of communication for humans. By providing a means to interact with technology through spoken language, voice-controlled interfaces tap into our innate ability to express ourselves vocally. This naturalness makes the interfaces more accessible and user-friendly, reducing the learning curve associated with traditional input methods such as typing or clicking.

The hands-free operation offered by voice-controlled interfaces is another significant advantage. Users can interact with devices or systems without the need for physical touch or manipulation, freeing their hands to perform other tasks simultaneously. This hands-free capability is particularly valuable in scenarios where manual input is challenging, such as when driving, cooking, or operating machinery. Voice-controlled interfaces enhance convenience and safety by allowing users to access information, control devices, or perform actions without diverting their attention away from the task at hand.

Voice-controlled interfaces also have the potential to enhance accessibility and inclusivity. They provide an alternative mode of interaction for individuals with mobility impairments or conditions that limit the use of traditional input devices. By leveraging voice commands, these interfaces enable users to overcome physical barriers and participate fully in the digital realm, empowering a broader range of users to engage with technology on their own terms.

Moreover, voice-controlled interfaces offer seamless integration with other smart devices and virtual assistants, enabling users to control and interact with their interconnected environments through voice commands. From adjusting lighting and temperature to playing music or searching for information, these interfaces provide a seamless and intuitive means of controlling and accessing various digital services and functionalities. The potential for integration with artificial intelligence and machine learning algorithms further enhances the capabilities and responsiveness of voice-controlled interfaces.

Voice-controlled interfaces are finding applications in diverse domains, including smart homes, automotive systems, customer service, healthcare, and more. As natural language processing technologies continue to advance, the accuracy, speed, and reliability of voice recognition are improving, further enhancing the user experience.

In the subsequent chapters, we will delve deeper into the implementation, challenges, and future possibilities of voice-controlled interfaces. By understanding and harnessing the potential of voice-controlled interactions, we can unlock new avenues for user empowerment, accessibility, and seamless integration of technology into our daily lives. Together, let us explore the exciting potential of voice-controlled interfaces and their role in shaping the next generation of user interfaces.

D. Haptic feedback and tactile interfaces

Haptic feedback and tactile interfaces have emerged as promising technologies that aim to enhance user experiences by incorporating the sense of touch into interactions with technology. This section explores the concept of haptic feedback and tactile interfaces and highlights their potential to revolutionize user interfaces and bring a new level of immersion and realism to human-computer interaction.

Haptic feedback refers to the use of touch-based sensations to provide users with physical feedback in response to their interactions. Tactile interfaces, on the other hand, encompass the design and implementation of interfaces that enable users to physically interact with virtual or augmented objects through touch or force feedback. Together, these technologies offer the potential to create more engaging and realistic user experiences.

One of the key advantages of haptic feedback and tactile interfaces is their ability to provide a sense of presence and immersion. By incorporating touch sensations into interactions, these interfaces bridge the gap between the virtual and physical worlds, allowing users to feel and manipulate virtual objects with a heightened sense of realism. This sense of presence can enhance the overall user experience, making interactions more engaging, memorable, and satisfying.

Haptic feedback and tactile interfaces also offer the advantage of enhanced feedback and guidance. Traditional screen-based interfaces often lack tactile cues that help users understand the consequences of their actions or the properties of virtual objects. By introducing haptic feedback, users can receive physical feedback and cues that provide valuable information about the interaction, such as texture, resistance, or spatial positioning. This additional feedback can reduce errors, improve precision, and enable users to make more informed decisions.

Moreover, haptic feedback and tactile interfaces have the potential to enhance accessibility. By incorporating touch-based feedback, these interfaces can provide alternative means of interaction for individuals with visual impairments or those who benefit from a multi-modal approach to interaction. The tactile nature of these interfaces enables users to access information and interact with technology through touch, expanding the possibilities for inclusivity and empowering users with different abilities.

Tactile interfaces also hold promise in fields such as virtual reality, where the sense of touch can significantly enhance the level of immersion. By integrating force feedback, vibration, or other haptic sensations into virtual environments, users can feel the impact of virtual objects, sense their presence, and experience a more believable and engaging virtual reality.

The implementation of haptic feedback and tactile interfaces involves various technologies, including vibrotactile actuators, force sensors, and shape-changing materials. As these technologies continue to advance, the capabilities and precision of haptic feedback and tactile interfaces are expanding, paving the way for more sophisticated and realistic touch-based interactions.

In the subsequent chapters, we will delve deeper into the implementation, challenges, and potential applications of haptic feedback and tactile interfaces. By understanding and harnessing the advantages of touch-based interactions, we can unlock new dimensions of user experiences, enhance accessibility, and create interfaces that are more intuitive, immersive, and user-centric. Together, let us explore the exciting potential of haptic feedback and tactile interfaces and their role in shaping the next generation of user interfaces.

Chapter 3
Augmented Reality and Mixed Reality Interfaces

A. Understanding augmented reality and mixed reality concepts

Augmented reality (AR) and mixed reality (MR) have emerged as transformative technologies that bridge the gap between the physical and digital worlds. This chapter explores the concepts of augmented reality and mixed reality interfaces, shedding light on their fundamental principles and their potential to revolutionize user interfaces and human-computer interaction.

Augmented reality involves overlaying digital content onto the real-world environment, seamlessly blending virtual elements with the physical surroundings. By leveraging computer vision, sensors, and wearable devices, augmented reality interfaces enable users to perceive and interact with virtual objects in real-time. These virtual elements can range from 2D images and text to 3D models and animations, enhancing the user's perception and understanding of the world.

Mixed reality, on the other hand, takes the concept of augmented reality a step further by enabling virtual objects to interact with the physical environment and vice versa. Mixed reality interfaces seamlessly integrate virtual and real elements, creating a hybrid environment where users can interact with and manipulate both digital and physical objects. This integration adds depth and interactivity to the user experience, opening up new possibilities for collaboration, creativity, and exploration.

One of the key advantages of augmented reality and mixed reality interfaces is their ability to provide contextually relevant information in real-time. By overlaying digital content onto the user's view of the real world, these interfaces can enhance understanding, facilitate decision-making, and provide valuable insights. For example, in industrial settings, workers can receive real-time instructions or visual cues overlaid onto the physical equipment, improving efficiency and reducing errors.

Another advantage is the potential for immersive and interactive experiences. Augmented reality and mixed reality interfaces enable users to interact with virtual objects as if they were part of the physical environment. Users can manipulate and explore 3D models, interact with virtual characters, or engage in immersive simulations. This level of interactivity enhances engagement, enables hands-on learning experiences, and opens up new avenues for entertainment, training, and design.

Furthermore, augmented reality and mixed reality interfaces have the potential to reshape user interfaces by freeing interactions from traditional screen-based constraints. Users can interact with digital content in a more natural and spatially aware manner, leveraging gestures, voice commands, or physical movements. This shift from 2D screens to a spatial interface allows for more intuitive and immersive interactions, reducing the cognitive load associated with traditional interfaces and enabling users to leverage their physical and spatial intelligence.

Augmented reality and mixed reality interfaces find applications in diverse fields, including gaming, education, healthcare, architecture, and industrial training. They offer the potential to enhance visualization, collaboration, and understanding in complex domains, empowering users with new ways to interact with information and the physical world.

In the subsequent chapters, we will delve deeper into the implementation, challenges, and potential applications of augmented reality and mixed reality interfaces. By understanding and harnessing the power of these technologies, we can unlock new dimensions of user experiences, transform industries, and shape the future of human-computer interaction. Together, let us explore the exciting potential of augmented reality and mixed reality interfaces and their role in shaping the next generation of user interfaces.

B. Exploring their impact on user interfaces

Augmented reality (AR) and mixed reality (MR) interfaces have the potential to revolutionize the way we interact with technology, bringing profound changes to user interfaces. This section explores the impact of AR and MR on user interfaces and highlights the transformative effects these technologies can have on human-computer interaction.

One of the key impacts of AR and MR interfaces is the shift from traditional screen-based interfaces to spatial interfaces. With AR and MR, digital content is seamlessly integrated into the physical environment, allowing users to interact with virtual objects in real-time. This spatial interface removes the limitations imposed by screens, enabling more natural, intuitive, and immersive interactions. Users can navigate through information and digital content as if they were interacting with physical objects, leveraging their spatial awareness and physical intelligence.

Another impact is the ability to personalize and contextualize user interfaces. AR and MR interfaces have the potential to provide highly tailored experiences by overlaying contextually relevant information onto the user's view. Users can receive real-time instructions, annotations, or recommendations based on their location, preferences, or the objects they are interacting with. This level of personalization enhances usability and efficiency, allowing users to access relevant information precisely when and where they need it.

Furthermore, AR and MR interfaces can enhance collaboration and communication. These technologies enable multiple users to share a mixed reality space and interact with virtual objects together. This opens up new possibilities for remote collaboration, where users can collaborate on projects, manipulate shared virtual objects, or conduct virtual meetings regardless of their physical location. The ability to see and interact with virtual content in a shared space promotes collaboration, improves understanding, and enhances teamwork.

AR and MR interfaces also have the potential to enhance visualization and understanding of complex data. Users can visualize data in three-dimensional space, making it easier to grasp complex relationships and patterns. This capability has significant implications for industries such as architecture, engineering, and data analytics, where visualizing and interacting with complex data sets can lead to more informed decision-making and improved insights.

Moreover, AR and MR interfaces can enhance accessibility by providing alternative modes of interaction for individuals with disabilities or impairments. These interfaces can offer features such as text-to-speech conversion, voice commands, or visual cues, enabling users with diverse abilities to access and interact with digital content. By prioritizing inclusivity and accessibility, AR and MR interfaces can empower a broader range of users to engage with technology and participate fully in the digital realm.

In summary, AR and MR interfaces have the potential to transform user interfaces by introducing spatial interactions, personalized experiences, collaboration, enhanced visualization, and improved accessibility. These technologies offer new ways to interact with information, digital content, and the physical world, paving the way for more natural, intuitive, and immersive user experiences. As AR and MR continue to evolve, their impact on user interfaces will shape the future of human-computer interaction, unlocking new possibilities and empowering users to interact with technology in unprecedented ways.

C. Applications and potential use cases of AR and MR interfaces

Augmented reality (AR) and mixed reality (MR) interfaces have a wide range of applications across various industries and domains. This section explores the applications and potential use cases of AR and MR interfaces, highlighting their transformative potential in enhancing user experiences and revolutionizing specific fields.

❖ Education and Training: AR and MR interfaces can revolutionize education by providing immersive and interactive learning experiences. Students can visualize complex concepts in three-dimensional space, interact with virtual objects, and engage in simulations that enhance understanding and retention. Additionally, AR and MR interfaces can facilitate training in fields such as healthcare, aviation, and engineering, offering realistic and safe environments for hands-on practice and skill development.

❖ Gaming and Entertainment: AR and MR interfaces offer exciting opportunities for gaming and entertainment. Users can engage in augmented reality gaming, where virtual elements are overlaid onto the real world, creating interactive and immersive experiences. Additionally, mixed reality interfaces enable users to become part of the game by integrating virtual characters and objects into the user's physical environment, blurring the boundaries between the real and virtual worlds.

❖ Design and Visualization: AR and MR interfaces have transformative potential in design and visualization industries. Architects and designers can use these interfaces to visualize and present virtual models of buildings or products in real-world contexts, enabling clients to experience designs before they are built. Additionally, AR and MR interfaces can aid in spatial planning, allowing users to overlay virtual elements onto physical spaces to explore different design options.

❖ Healthcare and Medicine: AR and MR interfaces have promising applications in healthcare and medicine. Surgeons can benefit from real-time visual overlays during procedures, providing guidance, highlighting important structures, and displaying vital information. Medical training can be enhanced through realistic simulations, allowing students to practice complex procedures in a virtual environment. AR and MR interfaces can also aid in rehabilitation by providing interactive visual feedback and guidance for patients.

❖ Manufacturing and Maintenance: AR and MR interfaces have the potential to transform manufacturing processes and maintenance operations. Assembly line workers can benefit from AR overlays that provide step-by-step instructions or highlight potential issues. Maintenance technicians can use AR and MR interfaces to access real-time information and digital manuals, simplifying complex repair procedures and reducing downtime.

❖ Retail and E-commerce: AR and MR interfaces offer unique opportunities in the retail and e-commerce industry. Customers can use AR interfaces to visualize products in their real-world environment before making a purchase. Virtual try-on experiences enable users to see how clothing or accessories would look on them without physically trying them on. AR and MR interfaces can enhance the shopping experience by providing interactive and personalized product information, reviews, and recommendations.

These are just a few examples of the wide-ranging applications and potential use cases of AR and MR interfaces. As these technologies continue to advance, their impact across industries will expand, providing new opportunities for innovation, engagement, and productivity. The possibilities of AR and MR interfaces are limited only by our imagination, and their integration into various domains will shape the future of human-computer interaction.

Chapter 4
Brain-Computer Interfaces

A. Introduction to brain-computer interfaces (BCIs)

Brain-computer interfaces (BCIs) represent a groundbreaking field at the intersection of neuroscience and technology, offering the potential to directly connect the human brain with external devices. This chapter serves as an introduction to BCIs, exploring their fundamental concepts and highlighting their transformative potential in the realm of user interfaces and human-computer interaction.

BCIs establish a direct communication pathway between the brain and external devices, allowing individuals to control and interact with technology using neural signals. These signals are detected and decoded through various methods, such as electroencephalography (EEG), functional magnetic resonance imaging (fMRI), or invasive techniques like implanted electrodes. Once the neural activity is captured, advanced algorithms analyze and interpret the signals to derive meaningful commands or actions.

One of the key advantages of BCIs is their potential to provide an alternative mode of interaction for individuals with severe motor disabilities or conditions that limit their ability to use traditional input devices. By directly tapping into the brain's neural activity, BCIs can bypass the need for physical movement and enable individuals to control assistive technologies, prosthetic devices, or even interact with virtual environments using their thoughts.

BCIs offer a wide range of potential applications across different domains. In the medical field, BCIs can be used for neurorehabilitation, enabling patients with motor impairments to regain movement or enhance their communication abilities. BCIs also hold promise in the field of neuroprosthetics, allowing amputees to control prosthetic limbs with greater dexterity and naturalness. Additionally, BCIs have the potential to enhance the quality of life for individuals with neurodegenerative diseases or locked-in syndrome, providing a means of communication and interaction that was previously inaccessible.

Beyond medical applications, BCIs can revolutionize the way we interact with technology in various domains. They hold potential for enhancing gaming experiences by enabling direct brain control in virtual reality environments, introducing new levels of immersion and interactivity. BCIs can also play a role in cognitive augmentation, aiding in memory enhancement, attention regulation, or decision-making processes.

While BCIs present exciting possibilities, there are still significant challenges to overcome. Signal quality, noise reduction, calibration, and user training are areas that require ongoing research and development. Additionally, ethical considerations, privacy concerns, and ensuring the safety and security of neural data are essential aspects that need careful attention.

In the subsequent chapters, we will delve deeper into the implementation, challenges, and potential applications of BCIs. By understanding and harnessing the power of BCIs, we can unlock new dimensions of human-computer interaction, empower individuals with disabilities, and explore the frontiers of neuroscience and technology. Together, let us embark on a journey to uncover the vast potential of brain-computer interfaces and their role in shaping the future of user interfaces.

B. How BCIs can revolutionize user interactions

Brain-computer interfaces (BCIs) have the potential to revolutionize the way we interact with technology, opening up new frontiers in user interfaces and human-computer interaction. This section explores the transformative capabilities of BCIs and highlights how they can revolutionize user interactions in profound ways.

One of the key ways BCIs can revolutionize user interactions is by providing a direct and intuitive means of communication and control. Traditional user interfaces often require manual input or specific gestures to interact with technology. BCIs offer a more seamless and natural approach by allowing users to control devices or systems using their thoughts. This direct brain control bypasses the need for physical movement, enabling individuals to interact with technology effortlessly and with greater speed and precision.

BCIs also have the potential to enhance accessibility and inclusivity. For individuals with severe motor disabilities or conditions that limit their ability to use traditional input devices, BCIs offer a lifeline by enabling them to regain independence and engage with technology on equal footing. BCIs can empower individuals with disabilities by providing them with a means of communication, control, and interaction that aligns with their thoughts and intentions, bridging the gap between their minds and the external world.

Moreover, BCIs hold the promise of expanding our cognitive capabilities. By leveraging neurofeedback and brainwave analysis, BCIs can provide real-time insights into our mental states and cognitive processes. This feedback can be used to enhance cognitive functions, such as attention regulation, memory enhancement, or mental focus. BCIs can assist individuals in achieving optimal cognitive states, leading to improved performance in various domains, including education, work, and creative endeavors.

BCIs can also enable immersive experiences by leveraging brain activity to adapt and respond to user needs. For example, in virtual reality environments, BCIs can detect the user's engagement level or emotional state and dynamically adjust the content or the virtual environment accordingly. This level of personalization and adaptability enhances immersion, making virtual experiences more responsive and tailored to individual preferences and needs.

Additionally, BCIs can enable novel forms of interaction and collaboration. Multiple individuals equipped with BCIs can establish brain-to-brain interfaces, allowing for direct communication and information exchange without the need for verbal or physical actions. This has the potential to transform fields such as teamwork, education, and gaming, where seamless and instant communication can enhance coordination, learning, and social interactions.

While BCIs are still in their early stages of development, their potential to revolutionize user interactions is immense. As the technology advances, the possibilities for BCIs to enhance communication, accessibility, cognitive augmentation, immersion, and collaboration will expand further, unlocking new frontiers in human-computer interaction.

In the subsequent chapters, we will delve deeper into the implementation, challenges, and potential applications of BCIs. By understanding and harnessing the power of BCIs, we can revolutionize the way we interact with technology, empower individuals, and pave the way for a future where our thoughts seamlessly shape the digital world around us. Together, let us embark on a journey to explore the transformative potential of brain-computer interfaces and their role in shaping the future of user interfaces.

C. Ethical considerations and challenges of BCIs

As brain-computer interfaces (BCIs) continue to advance, it is crucial to address the ethical considerations and challenges that accompany this transformative technology. This section explores the ethical considerations and challenges of BCIs, highlighting the importance of responsible development and use.

One of the primary ethical considerations is the privacy and security of neural data. BCIs gather highly sensitive information about an individual's neural activity, thoughts, and intentions. Safeguarding this data is essential to protect the individual's privacy and prevent unauthorized access. Developers and researchers must establish robust security measures and encryption protocols to ensure that neural data remains confidential and is used solely for its intended purposes.

Informed consent is another vital ethical aspect. Individuals who choose to use BCIs should have a clear understanding of the risks, benefits, and limitations of the technology. Informed consent should be obtained, ensuring that users are fully aware of how their neural data will be collected, stored, and used. Transparent communication and ongoing education about BCIs are crucial in empowering users to make informed decisions about their participation.

The potential for unintended consequences and misuse of BCIs raises ethical concerns. As BCIs gain more capabilities, there is a need to establish guidelines and regulations to prevent potential abuse. Ensuring responsible development and use of BCIs requires considering the potential risks and addressing issues related to unauthorized access, manipulation of neural data, or malicious use of brain-controlled systems. Ethical frameworks and guidelines should be established to guide developers, researchers, and users in their responsible use of BCIs.

Equity and accessibility are ethical considerations that must be addressed. BCIs should be developed with inclusivity in mind, ensuring that individuals with diverse abilities have equal access to the benefits of this technology. Efforts should be made to reduce any potential biases, limitations, or barriers that may disproportionately affect certain populations. BCIs should be designed to enhance accessibility, independence, and quality of life for all individuals, regardless of their background or physical abilities.

BCIs also raise ethical questions regarding cognitive enhancement and the potential for altering or manipulating brain function. The use of BCIs for cognitive enhancement purposes should be approached with caution, considering the potential risks and unintended consequences. Ethical guidelines should be established to ensure that cognitive enhancement technologies are used responsibly, with consideration for long-term effects, potential inequalities, and preserving the autonomy and well-being of individuals.

Lastly, the ethical challenges of BCIs include the need for rigorous scientific validation and transparency. As BCIs continue to evolve, it is crucial to maintain scientific rigor in the research and development processes. Transparent reporting of results, sharing of methodologies, and open collaboration within the scientific community are essential for ensuring the credibility, reproducibility, and reliability of BCI research.

In navigating the ethical considerations and challenges of BCIs, collaboration between various stakeholders, including researchers, developers, policymakers, ethicists, and users, is crucial. Ethical frameworks, guidelines, and regulations should be developed and regularly updated to adapt to the evolving landscape of BCIs, fostering responsible development, deployment, and use.

In the subsequent chapters, we will further explore the ethical considerations, challenges, and potential solutions surrounding BCIs. By addressing these ethical dimensions, we can ensure that BCIs are developed and utilized in a manner that upholds the values of privacy, consent, equity, accessibility, and responsible innovation. Together, let us navigate the ethical landscape of BCIs and pave the way for their ethical integration into user interfaces and human-computer interaction.

Chapter 5
The Internet of Things and Smart Environments

A. Role of IoT in shaping user interfaces

The Internet of Things (IoT) has revolutionized the way we interact with technology and our surrounding environments. This chapter explores the role of IoT in shaping user interfaces and highlights its transformative impact on user experiences and human-computer interaction.

IoT refers to the network of interconnected physical devices, objects, and sensors that collect and exchange data over the internet. These devices can range from everyday objects such as thermostats, appliances, and wearables to complex systems like smart cities and industrial infrastructure. IoT technology enables seamless communication, data exchange, and automation, creating smart environments that respond to user needs and preferences.

One of the key roles of IoT in shaping user interfaces is the integration of diverse devices and systems into a cohesive ecosystem. IoT enables the interconnectivity of devices, allowing them to communicate, share data, and collaborate. This interconnectedness extends to user interfaces, where users can control and interact with multiple devices and systems through unified interfaces. IoT brings together disparate technologies and streamlines the user experience, creating a seamless and integrated environment for users to interact with various interconnected devices.

Another aspect of IoT's role in user interfaces is the shift towards more intuitive and context-aware interactions. IoT devices and sensors collect vast amounts of data about the environment, user behavior, and preferences. This data can be leveraged to create personalized and context-aware user interfaces. For example, smart homes can adjust lighting, temperature, and music preferences based on user habits and preferences, creating a personalized and comfortable living environment. Context-aware interfaces enhance usability and convenience by anticipating user needs and providing relevant information and controls.

Moreover, IoT opens up opportunities for proactive and anticipatory user interfaces. Through data analytics and machine learning algorithms, IoT systems can learn user patterns, anticipate user needs, and automate certain tasks or processes. For example, wearable devices can monitor health data and provide timely notifications or recommendations to improve well-being. Proactive interfaces simplify user interactions, reduce cognitive load, and enhance productivity by taking on routine or repetitive tasks, allowing users to focus on more meaningful activities.

IoT also enables remote and ubiquitous access to user interfaces. With IoT, users can control and monitor devices and systems from anywhere, at any time, using mobile applications or web interfaces. This remote access offers convenience, flexibility, and peace of mind, empowering users to stay connected and in control even when they are away from their physical environments.

The role of IoT in user interfaces extends beyond individual devices and environments. It has the potential to facilitate seamless interactions across multiple domains, such as smart cities, transportation systems, healthcare networks, and industrial infrastructures. IoT enables the integration of these diverse systems into a unified user interface, enhancing efficiency, sustainability, and quality of life on a larger scale.

In the subsequent chapters, we will delve deeper into the implementation, challenges, and potential applications of IoT in user interfaces. By understanding and harnessing the role of IoT, we can create user-centric interfaces that seamlessly integrate technology into our daily lives, foster context-awareness, and empower users with greater control, convenience, and efficiency. Together, let us explore the transformative potential of IoT in shaping user interfaces and human-computer interaction.

B. Designing interfaces for smart homes and cities

The emergence of the Internet of Things (IoT) has paved the way for smart homes and cities, where interconnected devices and systems create intelligent environments that enhance efficiency, convenience, and sustainability. This section explores the design principles and considerations for creating interfaces that cater to the unique needs and interactions within smart homes and cities.

Designing interfaces for smart homes and cities requires a user-centric approach that considers the diverse range of devices, systems, and user preferences. Here are some key principles to guide the design process:

❖ Seamlessness: Interfaces should seamlessly integrate different devices and systems within the smart home or city ecosystem. Users should be able to control and interact with multiple devices through unified interfaces, reducing complexity and enabling a cohesive user experience. Designers should prioritize consistency, ensuring that interfaces maintain a common visual language and interaction patterns across various devices and systems.

❖ Context-awareness: Smart homes and cities generate vast amounts of data from sensors, devices, and user interactions. Interfaces should leverage this contextual information to deliver personalized and relevant experiences. For example, a smart home interface can adjust lighting, temperature, and entertainment preferences based on user habits, time of day, or occupancy. Designers should explore ways to capture and utilize contextual data to provide tailored and adaptive interfaces.

❖ Simplicity and clarity: In complex smart environments, interfaces should be designed to simplify interactions and minimize cognitive load. Clear and concise interfaces that prioritize essential information and controls promote usability and reduce user frustration. Visual hierarchy, intuitive navigation, and contextual help can assist users in understanding and navigating the interface efficiently.

❖ Remote access and mobile interfaces: Smart homes and cities often require remote access, allowing users to control and monitor their environments from anywhere. Designers should consider the design constraints and opportunities presented by mobile devices when designing remote interfaces. Mobile interfaces should be responsive, efficient, and provide relevant information and controls in a compact and accessible format.

❖ Feedback and transparency: Interfaces should provide feedback to users regarding the state of devices, actions taken, and system responses. Feedback mechanisms such as visual cues, notifications, or haptic feedback help users understand the impact of their actions and ensure a sense of control and trust. Transparent interfaces that provide clear information about data usage, privacy settings, and system behavior are crucial to building user trust in smart environments.

❖ Accessibility and inclusivity: Designing interfaces for smart homes and cities should prioritize accessibility for users with diverse abilities and needs. Interfaces should consider factors such as font size, color contrast, and support for assistive technologies to ensure that all users can interact with the technology effectively. Inclusive design practices can enhance the usability and accessibility of smart environments, enabling a broader range of users to benefit from the technology.

Designing interfaces for smart homes and cities is an ongoing process that requires iterative user feedback, continuous improvement, and adaptation to evolving technologies. By embracing user-centric design principles and considering the unique characteristics of smart environments, designers can create interfaces that empower users, simplify interactions, and enhance the overall experience within smart homes and cities.

In the subsequent chapters, we will delve deeper into the implementation, challenges, and potential applications of smart home and city interfaces. By understanding and applying these design principles, we can shape user interfaces that seamlessly integrate IoT technologies, foster convenience and sustainability, and create intelligent environments that improve our quality of life. Together, let us explore the transformative potential of designing interfaces for smart homes and cities in the context of the Internet of Things.

C. Challenges and opportunities in IoT-based interfaces

The proliferation of the Internet of Things (IoT) has presented both challenges and opportunities in the design and implementation of interfaces for smart environments. This section explores the key challenges and opportunities that arise when designing IoT-based interfaces for smart homes and cities.

❖ Interoperability and Integration: One of the significant challenges in IoT-based interfaces is ensuring interoperability and seamless integration of diverse devices and systems. With a wide array of manufacturers and protocols, achieving compatibility and standardization can be complex. Designers need to consider ways to bridge the gap between different devices, enabling them to communicate and collaborate effectively. Integration platforms, standardization efforts, and open APIs can help streamline interoperability and enable unified user experiences.

❖ Complexity and Cognitive Load: IoT-based interfaces often involve a multitude of interconnected devices and systems, which can introduce complexity and increase cognitive load for users. Designers must carefully consider how to simplify interactions, minimize cognitive load, and reduce the effort required to understand and control the smart environment. Visual hierarchy, contextual cues, and intuitive controls can help users navigate and manage the complexity, enhancing usability and user satisfaction.

❖ Data Privacy and Security: IoT-based interfaces rely on the collection and exchange of sensitive data, raising concerns about privacy and security. Designers must prioritize the protection of user data and ensure secure communication between devices and systems. Implementing strong encryption, authentication mechanisms, and user-friendly privacy settings are crucial to building trust and safeguarding user information.

❖ Scalability and Performance: As IoT ecosystems expand, interfaces need to accommodate the growing number of devices and data streams. Designers must consider the scalability and performance requirements of the interface to handle increased data volume and ensure real-time responsiveness. Efficient data processing, network optimization, and user-centered design can help maintain the performance of IoT-based interfaces as the system scales.

❖ User Empowerment and Control: IoT-based interfaces should empower users by providing them with control and visibility over their smart environments. Users should have the ability to customize settings, preferences, and automation rules, ensuring that the technology aligns with their individual needs and desires. Designers should strive to create interfaces that strike a balance between automation and user control, enabling users to feel empowered and engaged with their smart environments.

❖ Environmental Sustainability: IoT-based interfaces offer opportunities to promote environmental sustainability by optimizing resource consumption, energy efficiency, and waste reduction. Designers should consider ways to provide users with insights and controls that encourage eco-friendly behaviors, such as energy monitoring, adaptive lighting, and smart waste management. By fostering sustainability-conscious interfaces, IoT can contribute to creating greener and more sustainable smart environments.

These challenges also present opportunities for innovation and improvement. Designers can leverage advancements in machine learning, artificial intelligence, and data analytics to create intelligent interfaces that automate tasks, personalize experiences, and adapt to user preferences. User research, iterative design processes, and user feedback play vital roles in uncovering pain points and refining interfaces to meet user needs effectively.

In the subsequent chapters, we will delve deeper into the solutions and strategies for addressing the challenges in IoT-based interfaces. By embracing the opportunities and overcoming the challenges, designers can create interfaces that enhance the user experience, foster sustainable behaviors, and unlock the full potential of smart homes and cities powered by the Internet of Things. Together, let us explore the transformative possibilities and design pathways in IoT-based interfaces for smart environments.

Chapter 6
Adaptive and Context-Aware Interfaces

A. Importance of adaptive interfaces in personalized experiences

In an era of ever-evolving technologies and user preferences, adaptive interfaces play a crucial role in delivering personalized experiences that cater to individual needs and preferences. This chapter explores the importance of adaptive interfaces and their transformative impact on user experiences.

Adaptive interfaces are designed to dynamically adjust and respond to user interactions, preferences, and contextual factors. They have the ability to adapt their presentation, content, or behavior based on real-time data and insights. This adaptability enables interfaces to personalize the user experience, creating a tailored and customized interaction that resonates with each individual user.

One of the key benefits of adaptive interfaces is their ability to enhance usability and user satisfaction. By adapting to the user's preferences and habits, adaptive interfaces reduce the cognitive load associated with navigating and interacting with technology. Users are presented with relevant information, controls, and functionalities in a manner that aligns with their individual preferences, resulting in a more intuitive and efficient user experience.

Adaptive interfaces also foster engagement and immersion by tailoring content and interactions to the user's interests and goals. By leveraging user data, adaptive interfaces can provide personalized recommendations, suggestions, or notifications that resonate with the user's preferences and context. This personalization enhances user engagement, keeps users informed, and facilitates meaningful interactions that align with their specific needs.

Moreover, adaptive interfaces contribute to a sense of control and empowerment. By allowing users to customize their interfaces and preferences, adaptive systems empower individuals to shape their digital experiences according to their unique requirements and desires. Users feel more in control of their interactions, fostering a sense of ownership and personalization.

Adaptive interfaces are particularly valuable in dynamic and context-rich environments. By considering contextual factors such as location, time, device capabilities, and user preferences, adaptive interfaces can provide the most relevant and appropriate content and controls in each situation. For example, a mobile application may adapt its layout and functionality based on the user's location or the time of day, offering contextual recommendations or actions that align with the user's immediate needs.

Furthermore, adaptive interfaces have the potential to optimize performance and efficiency. By monitoring user behavior and system performance, adaptive interfaces can make intelligent adjustments to improve efficiency, responsiveness, and resource allocation. Adaptive interfaces can adapt to device capabilities, network conditions, or user constraints to provide optimal user experiences even in challenging contexts.

As technology continues to advance and user expectations evolve, the importance of adaptive interfaces in delivering personalized experiences will only grow. Adaptive interfaces have the potential to transform user interactions, fostering usability, engagement, control, and efficiency. By tailoring interfaces to individual needs and adapting to changing contexts, adaptive interfaces enable technology to seamlessly integrate into users' lives, offering experiences that are meaningful, relevant, and impactful.

In the subsequent chapters, we will delve deeper into the principles, techniques, and challenges of designing adaptive and context-aware interfaces. By understanding and embracing the power of adaptation, we can create interfaces that enhance personalization, optimize user experiences, and unlock the full potential of technology in meeting individual needs. Together, let us explore the transformative possibilities of adaptive interfaces and their role in shaping personalized experiences.

B. Context-awareness and its impact on user interfaces

Context-awareness is a fundamental aspect of adaptive interfaces, enabling user experiences that are tailored to specific situations and user needs. This section explores the importance of context-awareness and its transformative impact on user interfaces.

Context-awareness refers to the ability of interfaces to perceive and understand the surrounding environment, user behavior, and situational factors. By considering contextual information such as location, time, user preferences, device capabilities, and social or environmental conditions, context-aware interfaces can adapt their presentation, content, or behavior to deliver a more relevant and personalized user experience.

One of the key impacts of context-awareness on user interfaces is enhanced usability and efficiency. By leveraging contextual information, interfaces can anticipate user needs, reducing the effort required to locate information or perform tasks. For example, a context-aware mobile application can present relevant

79

options or actions based on the user's current location, saving users from having to manually search or configure settings. This targeted and streamlined approach enhances usability, making interfaces more intuitive and efficient.

Context-awareness also enables interfaces to provide timely and contextually relevant information. By analyzing contextual factors, interfaces can deliver personalized recommendations, notifications, or alerts that are tailored to the user's immediate situation or preferences. For instance, a smart assistant can provide weather updates, traffic information, or appointment reminders based on the user's location and schedule. This contextually driven information enhances the user experience by delivering precisely what the user needs at the right time and place.

Moreover, context-aware interfaces can adapt their presentation and behavior to suit different devices and contexts. With the proliferation of diverse devices such as smartphones, tablets, wearables, and smart appliances, interfaces need to be responsive and adaptable across these platforms. Context-awareness enables interfaces to adjust their layout, interactions, or content based on the device's screen size, input capabilities, or user preferences. This responsive design ensures a consistent and optimal user experience across different devices and contexts.

Another impact of context-awareness is the ability to provide intelligent automation and assistance. Interfaces can leverage contextual information to automate repetitive or routine tasks, relieving users from manual interactions. For example, a smart home interface can adjust temperature settings based on the time of day, occupancy, or user preferences without the need for explicit user input. Context-aware interfaces can also provide assistance by suggesting or initiating actions based on the user's context or historical patterns, reducing the cognitive load on the user and enhancing convenience.

Furthermore, context-awareness facilitates seamless integration with the physical environment. Interfaces can interact with and control IoT devices, sensors, or actuators in smart environments, offering users the ability to monitor and manage their surroundings. For instance, a context-aware interface can allow users to control lighting, security systems, or energy consumption based on occupancy or specific time-based rules. This integration between interfaces and the physical world creates a seamless and immersive user experience.

In conclusion, context-awareness has a transformative impact on user interfaces by enhancing usability, efficiency, relevance, and automation. By leveraging contextual information, interfaces can deliver personalized experiences, anticipate user needs, and seamlessly integrate with the physical environment. The continued advancements in technology and data analytics offer exciting opportunities for context-aware interfaces to further enhance user experiences, making interfaces more intelligent, intuitive, and tailored to individual needs.

In the subsequent chapters, we will delve deeper into the principles, techniques, and challenges of designing context-aware interfaces. By understanding and embracing context-awareness, we can create interfaces that adapt to user needs, deliver relevant information, and seamlessly integrate with the ever-evolving digital and physical landscapes. Together, let us explore the transformative possibilities of context-aware interfaces and their role in shaping user experiences.

C. Case studies of adaptive and context-aware interfaces

To illustrate the practical applications and transformative potential of adaptive and context-aware interfaces, this section presents case studies of real-world examples where these interfaces have been successfully implemented.

- ❖ Personalized News Aggregation: Many news aggregation platforms have embraced adaptive interfaces to deliver personalized news content to users. These interfaces consider various contextual factors, such as user preferences, reading habits, and browsing history, to curate a customized news feed.

By analyzing user interactions and feedback, these platforms adapt the content selection and presentation, ensuring that users receive articles and topics that align with their interests and preferences. The interfaces also allow users to provide explicit feedback on articles, further refining the system's understanding of individual preferences.

❖ Health and Fitness Tracking: Health and fitness applications often utilize adaptive and context-aware interfaces to provide personalized insights and guidance. These interfaces adapt to user behavior, goals, and contextual factors such as location, weather, and time of day. For example, a fitness tracking application may adjust activity recommendations based on the user's current location and weather conditions, suggesting indoor exercises on a rainy day. The interfaces also consider user preferences and historical data to offer personalized training plans, nutrition advice, and reminders, catering to individual needs and promoting healthier lifestyles.

❖ Smart Home Automation: Adaptive interfaces are commonly employed in smart home systems to provide intuitive control and automation. These interfaces analyze user routines, preferences, and contextual factors such as occupancy, time of day, and energy consumption patterns to automate various home functions. For instance, a smart home interface can automatically adjust lighting and temperature settings based on occupancy and time of day, providing convenience, energy efficiency, and personalized comfort. The interfaces allow users to customize automation rules and preferences, empowering them to shape their smart home experiences.

❖ Adaptive Learning Platforms: Educational platforms utilize adaptive and context-aware interfaces to personalize the learning experience for students. These interfaces analyze user performance, learning styles, and progress to dynamically adjust the content and difficulty level of educational materials. By adapting the presentation and pacing of the content, these interfaces provide tailored learning paths that cater to individual strengths, weaknesses, and preferences. The interfaces may also consider contextual factors such as time availability, device capabilities, and learning goals, optimizing the learning experience for each student.

❖ Smart Transportation Systems: Adaptive and context-aware interfaces are applied in smart transportation systems to enhance efficiency and user experiences. For example, ride-hailing applications adapt their interfaces based on user location, historical preferences, and real-time traffic conditions to provide accurate estimated arrival times and optimal routes. These interfaces also consider user preferences for car types, payment methods, and other customized settings. Additionally, public transportation applications may adjust the displayed routes, schedules, and service alerts based on the user's current location and selected preferences.

These case studies demonstrate the diverse applications and benefits of adaptive and context-aware interfaces across various domains. By tailoring experiences to individual needs, considering contextual factors, and dynamically adapting content and interactions, these interfaces provide personalized, efficient, and engaging user experiences.

In the subsequent chapters, we will further explore the principles, techniques, and challenges of designing adaptive and context-aware interfaces. By studying these case studies and understanding their underlying design principles, we can gain insights into the implementation and potential of these interfaces. Together, let us explore the transformative possibilities and learn from these real-world examples to create interfaces that adapt to user needs and contexts, delivering seamless and personalized user experiences.

Chapter 7
Future Directions and Possibilities

A. Speculating on the future of user interfaces

As technology continues to advance at an exponential pace, the future of user interfaces holds immense potential for transformation and innovation. This chapter delves into speculations about the future of user interfaces, exploring emerging trends and possibilities that could shape our interactions with technology.

❖ Natural Language and Conversational Interfaces: With the rapid advancements in natural language processing and machine learning, conversational interfaces are poised to become more prevalent in the future. Voice-controlled assistants and chatbots are already becoming increasingly sophisticated, allowing users to interact with technology through natural language conversations. In the future, these interfaces could evolve to understand complex queries, context, and emotions, enabling more seamless and intuitive interactions.

❖ Augmented and Virtual Reality Experiences: Augmented reality (AR) and virtual reality (VR) have the potential to revolutionize user interfaces by creating immersive and interactive experiences. AR overlays digital information onto the real world, while VR offers fully immersive simulated environments. In the future, AR and VR interfaces could seamlessly blend the digital and physical worlds, enabling users to interact with virtual objects and information in their natural environments, opening up new possibilities for gaming, education, communication, and more.

❖ Brain-Computer Interfaces (BCIs): BCIs have the potential to transform user interfaces by enabling direct communication between the human brain and technology. In the future, BCIs could become more refined and accessible, allowing users to control devices, applications, and systems using their thoughts alone. This could revolutionize accessibility, enhance cognitive abilities, and create entirely new ways of interacting with technology.

❖ Gesture and Motion Control: The rise of depth-sensing cameras and advanced motion tracking technologies has paved the way for gesture and motion-controlled interfaces. In the future, interfaces could become more responsive to subtle hand and body movements, allowing users to interact with technology in a more intuitive and natural way. Gesture recognition and tracking systems could enable precise control, enabling users to manipulate digital objects or navigate interfaces through gestures and motions.

❖ Biometric Interfaces: Biometric interfaces leverage unique physiological or behavioral characteristics of individuals for authentication and interaction. In the future, interfaces could incorporate biometric technologies such as facial recognition, fingerprint scanning, or even iris scanning to personalize and secure interactions. Biometric interfaces could offer seamless authentication, personalization, and enhanced security by leveraging the unique attributes of each individual.

❖ Wearable and Implantable Interfaces: As wearable technology becomes more sophisticated and miniaturized, it opens up possibilities for interfaces that seamlessly integrate into our daily lives. Future interfaces could be embedded in wearable devices such as smartwatches, smart glasses, or even smart clothing, enabling continuous and unobtrusive interactions. Furthermore, implantable interfaces could be developed, allowing direct communication between the human body and technology for enhanced capabilities or health monitoring.

❖ Multi-modal Interfaces: Future interfaces could combine various modes of interaction, such as touch, voice, gesture, and eye tracking, to create multi-modal experiences. These interfaces would leverage the strengths of each modality and offer users flexible and intuitive ways to interact with technology. For example, a user could speak a command, make a gesture, and glance at an object to perform complex tasks.

These speculations provide a glimpse into the exciting possibilities that lie ahead for user interfaces. While some of these technologies are still in their early stages, they hold great potential for transforming how we interact with technology in the future. As we continue to push the boundaries of innovation, it is essential to consider the ethical implications, user needs, and the impact these advancements will have on our daily lives.

In the subsequent chapters, we will explore these future directions in more detail, examining the challenges, opportunities, and potential applications they offer. By staying at the forefront of emerging trends and possibilities, we can shape the future of user interfaces in a way that enhances our interactions, empowers users, and creates meaningful and transformative experiences. Together, let us embark on this journey into the future of user interfaces.

B. Potential advancements and breakthroughs

The future of user interfaces holds immense potential for advancements and breakthroughs that could redefine our interactions with technology. This chapter explores some of the potential advancements and breakthroughs that may shape the future of user interfaces.

- ❖ Mind-Machine Integration: Advancements in brain-computer interface (BCI) technology could enable more seamless integration between the human mind and machines. In the future, we may see breakthroughs that allow users to control devices, interact with virtual environments, or even communicate with others using their thoughts alone. This level of mind-machine integration could revolutionize accessibility, empower individuals with disabilities, and open up entirely new possibilities for communication and control.
- ❖ Emotion Recognition and Response: As machine learning and artificial intelligence continue to evolve, interfaces may become more adept at recognizing and responding to human emotions. Advanced

emotion recognition algorithms could analyze facial expressions, tone of voice, and other biometric signals to gauge a user's emotional state. Interfaces could then adapt their responses, content, or interactions to better align with the user's emotions, enhancing empathy and personalization.

❖ Contextual Intelligence: Future interfaces may possess enhanced contextual intelligence, enabling them to understand and respond to a broader range of contextual factors. These interfaces could analyze data from various sensors, devices, and sources to infer the user's context, preferences, and intentions. By harnessing contextual intelligence, interfaces could deliver hyper-personalized experiences, anticipate user needs, and seamlessly adapt to dynamic environments.

❖ Human-like Interaction: Advancements in natural language processing, machine learning, and robotics may lead to interfaces that exhibit more human-like interaction capabilities. These interfaces could understand and respond to natural language conversations, exhibit empathy, and engage in nuanced interactions. Human-like interfaces could enhance social interactions, customer service experiences, and even assist in healthcare or therapy settings.

❖ Biometric Authentication and Security: The future of user interfaces may see advancements in biometric authentication and security measures. Interfaces could leverage biometric data, such as unique patterns in the iris, veins, or even DNA, to provide secure and seamless authentication. This could enhance privacy, eliminate the need for traditional passwords, and protect against unauthorized access.

❖ Holographic and Spatial Interfaces: Breakthroughs in display technologies may enable the development of holographic and spatial interfaces. These interfaces could project three-dimensional images, objects, or information into the user's physical environment, creating immersive and interactive experiences. Spatial interfaces could allow users to manipulate virtual objects in real space, navigate information-rich environments, and blur the boundaries between the physical and digital worlds.

❖ Collective Intelligence: The future of user interfaces may harness the power of collective intelligence, enabling interfaces to learn from and adapt to collective user behaviors and preferences. Interfaces could analyze vast amounts of aggregated user data, anonymized and protected for privacy, to deliver personalized recommendations, predictions, or collaborative decision-making support. By leveraging collective intelligence, interfaces could provide users with insights, suggestions, and knowledge that go beyond individual capabilities.

These potential advancements and breakthroughs offer a glimpse into the exciting future of user interfaces. While some of these ideas may still be in early stages or remain speculative, they highlight the transformative possibilities that lie ahead. As researchers, designers, and developers continue to push the boundaries of technology, it is important to balance innovation with ethical considerations, user needs, and societal impacts.

In the subsequent chapters, we will further explore these potential advancements and breakthroughs, examining their implications, challenges, and potential applications. By staying at the forefront of emerging technologies and envisioning future possibilities, we can shape user interfaces that enhance our interactions, empower users, and create meaningful and transformative experiences. Together, let us embark on this journey into the future of user interfaces.

C. Implications for user experience and human-computer interaction

As user interfaces continue to evolve, the future holds significant implications for user experience (UX) and human-computer interaction (HCI). This chapter explores the potential implications of future directions and possibilities on UX and HCI.

❖ Enhanced Personalization: Future interfaces have the potential to offer highly personalized experiences that cater to individual preferences, needs, and contexts. By leveraging advanced technologies such as artificial intelligence, machine learning, and user data analysis, interfaces can adapt and customize content, interactions, and recommendations. This enhanced personalization can lead to more engaging, efficient, and satisfying user experiences.

❖ Fluid Multimodal Interactions: With the emergence of new interface modalities such as gesture recognition, voice control, and eye tracking, future interfaces may facilitate fluid multimodal interactions. Users can seamlessly switch between different modes of interaction, choosing the most convenient or appropriate modality for specific tasks or contexts. This fluidity can provide users with a more natural and intuitive way to interact with technology, enhancing usability and reducing cognitive load.

❖ Natural Language Conversations: Advancements in natural language processing and understanding could enable interfaces to engage in more natural and human-like conversations. Users can interact with interfaces through spoken language, and the interfaces can interpret and respond contextually.

This shift towards conversational interfaces can enhance accessibility, simplify complex interactions, and foster more engaging and efficient communication.

❖ Ethical Considerations: As interfaces become more powerful and influential, ethical considerations become increasingly important. Future interfaces may raise concerns around data privacy, algorithmic biases, and the impact of persuasive design techniques. Designers and developers must navigate these ethical challenges by prioritizing transparency, consent, fairness, and inclusivity in interface design. Ethical guidelines and regulations will play a crucial role in ensuring responsible and user-centric interface development.

❖ Cognitive Load and Overload: While advanced interfaces can enhance user experiences, there is a risk of cognitive overload. Future interfaces that offer highly personalized, context-aware experiences may present users with an overwhelming amount of information, choices, or distractions. Designers must carefully manage cognitive load by prioritizing essential information, providing effective filtering and recommendation mechanisms, and minimizing distractions to maintain usability and prevent information overload.

❖ Empowerment and Autonomy: Future interfaces have the potential to empower users and enhance their sense of autonomy. By allowing users to personalize their interfaces, control their digital experiences, and make informed decisions, interfaces can foster a sense of ownership and agency. Empowering interfaces can lead to increased user satisfaction, engagement, and productivity.

❖ Evolving User Expectations: The rapid advancements in technology shape user expectations, creating a cycle of continuous improvement in user interfaces. As users become accustomed to more intelligent, adaptive, and immersive interfaces, their expectations for seamless, personalized, and context-aware experiences will continue to grow. Designers and developers must stay attuned to evolving user expectations and strive to exceed them to deliver compelling user experiences.

These implications highlight the profound impact that future user interfaces can have on UX and HCI. As technology advances, it is crucial to consider the user's needs, ethical considerations, and societal implications. By aligning future interface developments with human-centered principles, we can shape user experiences that are engaging, empowering, inclusive, and beneficial to individuals and society.

In the subsequent chapters, we will delve deeper into these implications, examining the challenges and opportunities they present. By understanding the implications for UX and HCI, we can navigate the future of user interfaces with a user-centric mindset, creating interfaces that enhance human abilities, enable meaningful interactions, and shape a positive and transformative technological landscape. Together, let us embrace the possibilities and strive for a future where interfaces empower and enrich our lives.

Conclusion

A. Recap of the next generation of user interfaces

Throughout this book, we have explored the exciting realm of the next generation of user interfaces. We have delved into the evolution of screens as primary interfaces, the limitations of current interfaces, and the need for innovative solutions. We have examined emerging technologies such as gesture-based interfaces, voice-controlled interfaces, haptic feedback, augmented reality, mixed reality, brain-computer interfaces, the Internet of Things, and adaptive interfaces. We have speculated on the future of user interfaces, including advancements and breakthroughs that could revolutionize human-computer interaction.

In recap, the next generation of user interfaces holds transformative potential for enhancing user experiences, personalization, and adaptability. Screens, which have been central to our interaction with technology, are being complemented by alternative interfaces that leverage natural interactions, contextual awareness, and personalized experiences. These interfaces cater to the diverse needs and preferences of users, adapting to their contexts and enabling more intuitive and efficient interactions.

We have explored the challenges and opportunities posed by these innovative interfaces. We have recognized the importance of usability, engagement, control, and ethical considerations in their design. We have examined case studies that demonstrate how these interfaces are already shaping various domains, from personalized news aggregation and health tracking to smart homes and transportation systems.

The future of user interfaces holds immense possibilities. We have speculated on advancements such as mind-machine integration, emotion recognition and response, contextual intelligence, human-like interaction, biometric authentication, holographic and spatial interfaces, and collective intelligence. These advancements have significant implications for user experience, human-computer interaction, personalization, multimodal interactions, ethics, cognitive load, empowerment, and evolving user expectations.

As we conclude this book, it is crucial to recognize that the next generation of user interfaces is an ongoing journey of innovation, refinement, and adaptation. It requires a user-centric mindset, continuous research, iterative design processes, and ethical considerations. The future of user interfaces is not solely about technology; it is about enhancing our interactions with technology to create meaningful, seamless, and transformative experiences.

By embracing the principles, techniques, and possibilities explored in this book, we can contribute to shaping the future of user interfaces. We can design interfaces that empower individuals, enhance accessibility, foster engagement, and create positive impacts on individuals and society. Let us strive for interfaces that seamlessly integrate with our lives, amplify our abilities, and foster a harmonious relationship between humans and technology.

As we move forward, let us continue to explore, innovate, and collaborate to unlock the full potential of the next generation of user interfaces. Together, we can shape a future where technology enriches our lives, connects us in meaningful ways, and enables us to navigate the digital landscape with ease and joy.

B. Importance of embracing new interface technologies

In this book, we have embarked on a journey to explore the next generation of user interfaces and the transformative possibilities they offer. As we conclude, it is crucial to emphasize the importance of embracing these new interface technologies for individuals, businesses, and society as a whole.

❖ Enhanced User Experiences: Embracing new interface technologies allows us to elevate user experiences to new heights. By leveraging emerging technologies such as gesture-based interfaces, voice-controlled interfaces, augmented reality, and adaptive interfaces, we can create interfaces that are more intuitive, personalized, and engaging. These technologies have the power to enhance usability, efficiency, and satisfaction, enabling users to seamlessly interact with technology in ways that feel natural and empowering.

❖ Innovation and Competitive Advantage: Embracing new interface technologies fosters innovation and provides a competitive edge for businesses. By staying at the forefront of interface advancements, organizations can differentiate themselves by delivering cutting-edge products and services. Forward-thinking businesses that embrace these technologies can anticipate user needs, create unique experiences, and shape the future of their industries.

❖ Accessibility and Inclusivity: New interface technologies have the potential to enhance accessibility and inclusivity in digital experiences. By designing interfaces that cater to diverse abilities and preferences, we can empower individuals with disabilities, elderly populations, and those with different learning styles. These technologies enable us to break down barriers and ensure that everyone can participate fully in the digital world.

❖ Transformative Solutions: Embracing new interface technologies opens doors to transformative solutions for complex challenges. By embracing technologies such as brain-computer interfaces, the Internet of Things, and adaptive interfaces, we can tackle issues in healthcare, education, sustainability, and more. These technologies enable us to create solutions that improve quality of life, enhance productivity, and address societal and environmental concerns.

❖ Future-Proofing: The landscape of technology is ever-evolving, and embracing new interface technologies is essential for future-proofing our digital experiences. By actively exploring and adopting emerging technologies, we can adapt to changing user expectations and technological advancements. This proactive approach allows us to be prepared for the future, harnessing the potential of new technologies as they emerge.

❖ Human-Technology Integration: Embracing new interface technologies facilitates a seamless integration of humans and technology. These interfaces enhance our natural abilities, augment our capabilities, and create harmonious interactions between humans and machines. By embracing these technologies, we can design interfaces that enhance human potential and empower individuals to leverage technology as a tool for creativity, productivity, and personal growth.

As we conclude this book, let us recognize the immense value of embracing new interface technologies. By embracing innovation, considering user needs, and being mindful of ethical considerations, we can shape a future where technology enriches our lives, fosters connectivity, and enables us to navigate the digital world with ease and joy.

Let us embrace the transformative possibilities of the next generation of user interfaces, leveraging their potential to enhance user experiences, drive innovation, foster accessibility, and address complex challenges.

Together, we can create a future where interfaces seamlessly integrate into our lives, empower individuals, and unlock the full potential of human-technology collaboration.

C. Exciting possibilities for the future of user interfaces

As we conclude this book on the next generation of user interfaces, we are filled with anticipation for the exciting possibilities that lie ahead. The future of user interfaces holds immense potential for transforming our interactions with technology and reshaping the way we live, work, and communicate. Let us explore some of the thrilling possibilities that await us.

❖ Immersive Experiences: The future of user interfaces promises immersive experiences that blur the boundaries between the physical and digital worlds. Augmented reality (AR) and virtual reality (VR) interfaces offer the potential for fully immersive and interactive environments, where users can explore virtual landscapes, manipulate digital objects, and engage in collaborative experiences. These interfaces create new avenues for entertainment, education, training, and even remote collaboration.

❖ Sensory-rich Interfaces: Advancements in haptic feedback, tactile interfaces, and multisensory technologies open up possibilities for interfaces that engage our senses beyond just sight and sound. Future interfaces could provide tactile feedback, simulate textures and surfaces, and even trigger olfactory or gustatory sensations. These sensory-rich interfaces enhance realism, emotional engagement, and accessibility for individuals with sensory impairments.

❖ Intelligent Assistance: The rise of artificial intelligence and machine learning fuels the development of intelligent assistant interfaces. These interfaces have the potential to understand context, anticipate user needs, and proactively assist users in various domains. Intelligent assistants can provide personalized recommendations, automate routine tasks, and offer proactive suggestions, becoming indispensable companions in our daily lives.

❖ Seamless Integration: The future holds the promise of interfaces seamlessly integrating into our surroundings and everyday objects. Internet of Things (IoT) interfaces enable interconnected devices to communicate and collaborate, creating smart environments that respond to our needs. Interfaces could be embedded in everyday objects, enabling intuitive interactions and personalized experiences. For example, our homes, cars, and even clothing could become smart interfaces that adapt to our preferences and facilitate effortless interactions.

❖ Ethical and Responsible Interfaces: As the field of user interfaces advances, there is an increasing focus on ethical considerations and responsible design. Future interfaces will prioritize privacy, transparency, and inclusivity, ensuring that users have control over their data and that technology respects their values and rights. Ethical interfaces will be designed to avoid biases, promote fairness, and contribute positively to the well-being of individuals and society.

❖ Collaborative and Cooperative Interfaces: The future of user interfaces embraces collaboration and cooperation between humans and machines. Interfaces could facilitate seamless collaboration between individuals, allowing real-time communication, co-creation, and information sharing. Cooperative interfaces can harness collective intelligence, enabling crowdsourcing, collaborative problem-solving, and collective decision-making.

❖ Mind-Computer Interfaces: Breakthroughs in brain-computer interfaces hold the potential for direct communication between the human brain and technology. In the future, interfaces could interpret and translate our thoughts, enabling us to control devices, access information, and communicate without physical interaction. This transformative technology has profound implications for accessibility, healthcare, and the understanding of human cognition.

These exciting possibilities for the future of user interfaces offer a glimpse into the transformative potential that lies ahead. By embracing innovation, considering user needs, and prioritizing ethical considerations, we can shape user interfaces that enhance our lives, enable meaningful interactions, and foster human potential.

As we conclude this book, let us embrace the thrilling possibilities of the future and strive to create user interfaces that are inclusive, empowering, and beneficial to individuals and society. By staying curious, adaptive, and open to new ideas, we can shape a future where interfaces seamlessly integrate into our lives, amplify our abilities, and foster a harmonious relationship between humans and technology.

Together, let us embark on this exciting journey into the future of user interfaces, harnessing their potential to enrich our lives, connect us in meaningful ways, and pave the way for a more vibrant and technologically advanced world.

www.ingramcontent.com/pod-product-compliance
Lightning Source LLC
LaVergne TN
LVHW022125060326
832903LV00063B/4032